Job Satisfaction
for Child and
Youth Care Workers
Third Edition

Mark A. Krueger, Ph.D.

CWLA Press ◆ Washington, DC

CWLA Press is an imprint of the Child Welfare League of America

© 1996 by the Child Welfare League of America, Inc. All rights reserved. Neither this book nor any part may be reproduced or transmitted in any form or by any means, electronic or mechanical, including photocopying, microfilming, and recording, or by any information storage and retrieval system, without permission in writing from the publisher. For information on this or other CWLA publications, contact the CWLA Publications Department at the address below.

CHILD WELFARE LEAGUE OF AMERICA, INC.

440 First Street, NW, Suite 310,
Washington, DC 20001-2085

Email: books@cwla.org

CURRENT PRINTING (last digit)
10 9 8 7 6 5 4 3 2 1

Cover design by Jennifer Geanakos
Text design by Eve Malakoff-Klein

Printed in the United States of America

ISBN # 0-87868-259-9

Contents

INTRODUCTION

Job satisfaction can be defined in several ways. It is a feeling of fulfillment or pleasure associated with one's work. It is also an attitude about various facets of a job, such as working conditions, supervision, and decision making.

Job satisfaction and job competence are interrelated. In other words, people who are satisfied with their jobs tend to perform better. They also tend to stay longer at their places of employment. Job satisfaction is extremely important in child and youth care work because children and families need competent, enthusiastic workers on whom they can count to be there.

This third edition of *Job Satisfaction* continues to promote satisfaction for child and youth care workers. The book is based on the premise that satisfaction comes from many inner personal sources and is nourished by supportive organizational practices, daily interactions, and career goals.

I have selected many quotes and created vignettes to illustrate key concepts in this book. These examples of best practice in a variety of community and group care programs for at-risk children and youths help highlight the actions and attitudes that I believe are major contributors to satisfaction.

1

PERSONAL SOURCES OF SATISFACTION

Satisfaction comes first and foremost from an inner calling or sense of purpose. People who are happy in child and youth care work are driven by a fire in their belly, a gut feeling, a mission to be with and help empower children.

> I always liked kids, then when I took my first job with disturbed children, I realized what an impact I could have with children who others had written off. [Powell 1989]

> I knew when I was nine years old that one day I would work with children... [Vander Ven 1990: 68]

> At age 18, this became my grand passion; I am no longer young, but it is still grand. [Brendtro 1991: 45]

Special Moments, Self-Discovery, and Sense of Purpose

When asked about their greatest sources of satisfaction, workers often recall special moments with children, the insight they gain about themselves, and the increasing sense of purpose they acquire from helping others.

Special Moments

Most workers can recall touching moments such as the following:

Now... now she lay there sleeping, breathing softly and evenly... I leaned over and pulled her rumpled covers over her arms, softly brushed the tussled hair from her face, and whispered, Good night Ana, see you in the morning. [Nault 1987: 86]

Leo, the Indian-looking boy, is watching TV in the lounge. I try to start a conversation with him. I sit down with him and put my arm around his shoulder. "Having a lazy day, eh?" I ask. He says "Yah." Then very naturally and gently he rests his head on my shoulder. I feel so touched. It's the soft feeling when something inside seems to be melting inside between the kids and me. [Phuc Ngyun 1992: 94] ·

As I looked down at him to say good-bye, he suddenly reached up and grabbed on me with his arms around my neck. "Norman, I don't want you to leave." [Powell 1990: 20]

Self-Discovery: Shared Journeys

Satisfied workers also often speak about the enlightenment and fulfillment that comes from self-discovery in child and youth care [Fewster 1990; Garfat 1991]. In describing child and youth care as a shared journey, Fewster wrote:

Child and youth care workers appear as fellow travelers along the pathway for an increasing number of children in our society. For brief periods of time they share part of their respective journeys... Those who journey with calm confidence and courage know that the possibilities and potentials are endless. [Fewster 1991: 85]

In expressing what she had gained from her work with severely abused children, Mary Jean Meyer wrote:

At the onset of my work with victimized children, I was willing to leave my early conflicts undisturbed. But when the children slowly and ... shyly, gave me permission to step into their inner worlds, without know-

ing it, they gave me a very special gift. A chance to recapture my own childhood from the mists of the past. [Meyer 1991: 83]

Sense of Purpose

In discussing the will to identity—the search to know and express oneself as part of one's community—Vaclav Havel wrote: "By perceiving ourselves as part of the river, we accept responsibility for the river as a whole" [1983: 301]. In this context, satisfied workers are part of the river of child and youth care. They find a sense of purpose or cause in what they do.

Their daily struggle within the minutiae of everyday life was also my own, in part for their sake, but I am sure also for my own and society's. How could I leave with so much yet to be learned and done? [Maier 1991: 53]

Additional Sources

There are numerous other sources of satisfaction in child and youth care, such as devising a novel way of doing something, solving a problem, achieving insight through a completely different way of looking at things, or discovering a new activity.

Baizerman [1992] refers to youth work as "improvised like jazz" and Beker [1991] calls it the "flow of life." At times, child and youth care is like modern dance. It can also be a pleasing conversation... a series of eye contacts... moments of silence... motions and words that string together.

Child and youth care is also inherently "good" work. There is a certain rapid pace and flow to it, followed by a sense of peaceful exhaustion. "Where else can you play and get paid for it?" we used to say.

For most workers, it seems that satisfaction comes from a mix of these factors and others. Child and youth care workers like what they do and are fulfilled by it. They get pleasure from learning about themselves and from experience. They enjoy the process of mastering their craft and sharing it with the children. They have fun. They feel good. They are charged by their involvement in activity and delighted by the acceptance they receive from their peers.

Characteristics of Satisfied Workers

Among satisfied workers, the following characteristics, attitudes, and actions are usually evident:

♦ They maintain their passion and commitment. Although their feelings change over time and they go through periods of highs and lows, they never forget their initial excitement or lose their desire to help.

Sometimes after a hard day, Jack wonders why he chose youth work. The pay is not good and the work is tiring and demanding. Beneath it all, though, he knows there is nothing else he would rather do or that would be more fulfilling. He is here because he wants to be. When he doubts himself, he talks to others and renews his commitment.

♦ They find satisfaction in small things: a smile, a quiet moment sitting together with a child, a youth combing his hair, a good try, an expressed feeling, making a bed, etc.

Ken records with excitement the following changes in his log notes. "Willy combed his hair for the first time. John said hello today instead of 'fuck you.' Tony and Maria played together for the first time without arguing."

♦ They learn from adversity and struggle. Unlike other workers who burn out or get bogged down in problems, satisfied workers view child and youth care work as a challenge in which they learn from successes and failures. They enjoy overcoming obstacles.

Greg has just finished breaking up a fight. The two boys are off to the side, cooling off. He is angry and still a bit frightened, but he is thinking already about how he will prevent it next time.

♦ Their alertness, awareness, movement, play, and interaction are enhanced by good physical health. They get lots of rest, eat well, and stay in shape.

Maria jogs three times a week before coming to work. In summer, she bikes on weekends and in winter she cross-country skis. She watches what she eats and gets the proper amount of sleep.

♦ They plan and prepare in advance to ensure positive interactions and outcomes.

Nadia comes in early to organize her day. She goes over her notes and thinks through what she wants to accomplish on her shift.

♦ They find enjoyment in learning about themselves and others, and from peers, clients, mentors, classes, workshops, books, and articles.

Erika listens to her colleagues and the children. She gets engaged in discussions that challenge her to think about herself and the way she does things. After hours, she tries to stay abreast of what's being written in journals and books. Whenever she can, she attends workshops. She's eager to learn as much as she can.

♦ They take pleasure in the process as well as the outcomes of interacting with children and families. They enmesh themselves in activities. They love the action.

On most days, Jeff can't wait to get to work. He likes to play, swim, work, joke, talk, and just hang out with the kids.

♦ They find fulfillment in carrying out and learning from decisions that they have helped make. They seek autonomy and consensus (see Chapter 3).

The team members at the neighborhood center like their autonomy. They enjoy making decisions about everything from daily activities to budgets. Sometimes, their decisions don't work out, but they are able to learn from their experiences.

♦ They view the achievement of short-term personal goals as part of their long-range plan of professional development (see Chapter 4).

Kathy has high expectations for herself and the children. She knows, however, that to achieve these expectations, she and they will have to go through a series of steps. Thus, she has developed a clear set of learning ob-jectives for herself and for the children.

♦ They laugh together, at themselves, and with the children and parents.

Often the workers at the center tell funny stories about their experiences. The humor provides the energy boost they need. There are many humorous events at work. They are careful, though, not to laugh at the children. They laugh with them and at themselves.

♦ They are assertive. They know what they want and have the capacity to articulate their wants in a fruitful manner.

"I've thought about how we can change our work schedule to better meet the needs of the children and allow us each a few more week-end hours off," Daniel says as he passes out the schedule he worked on for several days.

♦ They believe in and have tremendous pride in what they are doing.

Nick sweeps the floor at night and plays bas-ketball with the same enthusiasm he dis-plays when telling others about his job.

♦ They are open and approachable.

Mary listens intently as Louisa suggests that she try ignoring Tony when he is trying to distract her. "Okay," *Mary says.* "I think I'll try that. It sounds like a good idea."

♦ They leave their problems from work at work. They try to resolve disagreements or solve problems before they go home.

Pam walks over to Bill at the end of their shift. "Can we talk a minute?" *she asks.*

"Sure," *he responds.*

"When you jumped in when I was trying to discipline Alicia today, I was upset," *says Pam.* "I appreciate your willingness to help, but I'm trying to establish my own authority with the kids and that sort of thing undermines it. I think it would help in the future if you waited until I asked for help."

♦ Their lives outside of work are satisfying. They have many other interests.

On her day off, Linda spends time with her boyfriend or her sister. She also likes to read. She looks forward to her own time as much as, if not more than, the time she spends at work.

Increasing Satisfaction

If you want to increase your job satisfaction, consider the following suggestions:

1. Take time periodically to renew your commitment.

2. Savor special moments and learn as much as possible from interactions with children and your colleagues.

3. Talk to supervisors or experienced workers who seems to be enjoying what they are doing and watch and learn from them.

4. Pay attention to your physical health, stay in shape, and eat and sleep well.

5. Be prepared. Take a little extra time to plan.

6. Play. Become enmeshed in activity.

7. Challenge yourself. Learn a new skill, pursue new ideas, and be creative.

8. Go after what you want. Think it through, develop a constructive proposal, and try it!

9. Focus on the good moments with the kids and laugh with your colleagues.

10. Join a professional association and meet others who have made child and youth care their mission (see Chapter 5).

2

ORGANIZATIONAL SUPPORT

Personal satisfaction is enhanced by organizational attitudes and practices, such as those at "Raintree," a composite drawn from several agencies and described below.

Workers stay longer at the Raintree Center than those at most other centers. And they don't just stay, they grow together. As they interact with one another, they try to practice the same methods of care and support they use with the children and families. They listen, praise, and constructively criticize one another.

It's not easy to get a job at Raintree. All candidates go through a rigorous recruitment process.

Once a worker is hired, learning is a priority. In addition to an inservice program, workers are enrolled in college courses and are required to attend conferences and workshops.

Raintree has a step system. Workers who work hard and develop their skills are promoted and serve as mentors and role models for other workers. Workers at Raintree are paid wages comparable to those of social workers and teachers with equivalent amounts of experience and education. Although their salaries are low in comparison to other occupations, they are paid enough to meet their needs.

Each worker receives one-on-one supervision once a week from the supervisor and suggestions and support in team meetings from fellow team members. Like the one-on-ones and group meetings they have with the youths, the staff members view these supervisory times as a very important part of their growth. It is a time to solve problems and to explore new alternatives. Supervision is also a professional source of support that the workers look forward to each week. Realizing how stressful and demanding the work is, the supervisor encourages and praises the workers and helps them plan for the future.

Experienced workers serve as mentors to new workers. The experienced workers are positive role models and are enthusiastic about their work. They teach new workers as they work side by side with them.

Most decisions are made by consensus. Changes in agency philosophy, annual budgets, rules and policies for daily operation, and individual treatment, education, and care plans are all discussed together.

A worker-of-the-month award is given to a worker each month for outstanding performance. The award, along with a picture of the worker, is displayed in the main lobby.

Some workers stay for several years and serve as models and mentors. Others leave after two or three years, taking the skills they have learned, positive attitudes, and memories with them.

Finding the Right People

After she completes her bachelor's degree in social work with an emphasis on youth work, Natalie applies for a job at the youth center. She saw the announcement on the bulletin board at the placement office.

She is interviewed by the supervisor, other workers, and the director. They seem as interested in who she is as they are in how skilled she is. She also spends a day in the center with the kids and is given time to reflect on her experience and the center's phi-

losophy before she is made an offer, which she accepts.

The agency searches for people who have enthusiasm, compassion and many of the other attributes described in Chapter One—people who have the capacity to work hard, care, play, and spend time with youths. Candidates with a positive child and youth care experience and/or a bachelor's degree in a related human service area or from one of the undergraduate programs in child and youth care are preferred.

During the interviews, interviewers try to get to know the candidates as well as possible. They take their time. They also provide candidates with an accurate description of the agency philosophy and the struggles and joys of the job. Final candidates experience a shift or day with other workers and the children.

Screening tests are used to augment—not substitute for—personal opinions. Interviewers make the final decision by consensus, paying as much attention to their instincts as their intellects. During the interview, the candidate may be asked:

♦ Why have you chosen to enter child and youth care work?

♦ What is your philosophy of care?

♦ What special strengths do you believe you have for working with children?

♦ What special strengths do you have for working with other professionals?

♦ Do you like to play?

♦ Are you available to work varied hours?

♦ Will the salary be sufficient?

♦ Are you in good health?

♦ How well do you handle stress?

♦ What do you do to stay in shape? To handle stress?

♦ What kind of commitment can you make?

♦ What are your career plans?

Initial Experiences

For a period of several weeks, Natalie is assigned to work alongside of Akim, a skilled and enthusiastic youth worker. Later, she looks back at this experience as a time of tremendous learning and support.

New workers work with experienced, enthusiastic, competent workers until they develop the skills and confidence they need to work on their own. They also spend time (daily if possible) with supervisors and mentors discussing daily observations, solving problems, and exploring and questioning situations from several perspectives. The goal is to get everyone off to a good start.

Introductory Inservice

Natalie also attends 40 hours of inservice training during her first six months. This provides her with information and skills that are useful in overcoming many of her early difficulties and in helping her engage the youths in various productive activities.

New workers receive at least 40 hours of introductory training, spread over a period of weeks so the workers can relate the learning to their experience and explore how it can be integrated into practice. The topics include program operating procedures and many of the basic skills identified by the child and youth care profession [Krueger 1991].

Continuous Learning

Like Akim, Natalie seizes the opportunities to learn. The more she knows, the more competent she feels.

Learning is part of the organization's central mission. Members of the organization realize that they have to continue their education and that they must learn as much as possible from their colleagues and clients [Senge 1995].

Learning is emphasized in daily interactions, team meetings, and supervisory sessions. Role plays, cooperative learning (workers teaching workers), videotapes, team exchanges, problem-solving exercises, demonstration projects, and Friday afternoon rap sessions are just a few of the methods used to facilitate learning.

Support for learning includes partial reimbursement for college tuition, time to attend workshops, seminars, and conferences, and a comprehensive inservice training program. Workers and administrators plan the inservice curricula and learn together. Workers usually receive a minimum of 40 hours of inservice training a year (in addition to the introductory training provided by their employer.)

Step Plans/Promotional Systems

After three years of exceptional performance, Akim was promoted to Youth Worker II. In striving for this position, he was motivated by the increase in salary, as well as the status and increased responsibility that went with the new position. This gives Natalie hope that if she works hard and per-

forms, she will also receive the salary, sta-tus, and responsibility that go along with being a Youth Worker II.

Workers who perform well are rewarded with additional compensation and promo-tion to higher levels of direct line leadership and responsibility. This is accomplished in part with step plans and promotional sys-tems, which are designed to encourage workers to grow, to support them in devel-oping their skills, and to provide incentives and rewards for productivity.

Workers and administrators develop sys-tems of compensation and promotion to-gether, determining what skills, experi-ences, and training are most essential for improving the quality of service as well as for promoting staff growth and develop-ment. Several paths for advancement are created. For example, one worker with the basic competencies might be encouraged to develop the skills to be a shift leader, an-other might become a treatment team leader, and a third might be a leader in rec-reation programming.

Workers and administrators also imple-ment the systems together, empowering members of the organization to grow. Work-ers ask for what they need, and administra-tors and fellow workers try to accommodate by working with one another toward performance objectives. The goals are to have the most competent and talented people reach the top levels so they can lead and mentor new staff, and to develop a variety of skills and talents among workers.

Step systems usually include criteria such as those shown on pages 22 and 23.

Evaluation

Natalie and Akim receive a formal written evaluation every year, but they are rarely surprised at the results because their evaluation has been an ongoing process. At the center, evaluations are seen as another part of the continuous learning process, not as a way to check up on people.

Individual performance evaluation is ongoing. It is carried out through regularly scheduled individual and team supervision and with quantitative, as well as qualitative, assessments, which provide workers with helpful descriptions of their progress.

Evaluations often include assessments of the worker's ability to:

♦ carry out the mission of the organization;

♦ develop growth-producing relationships;

♦ assess needs, plan activities, and carry out strategies;

A Step System

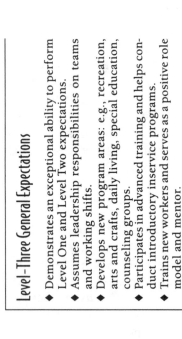

Level-Three General Expectations

- ◆ Demonstrates an exceptional ability to perform Level One and Level Two expectations.
- ◆ Assumes leadership responsibilities on teams and working shifts.
- ◆ Develops new program areas: e.g., recreation, arts and crafts, daily living, special education, counseling groups.
- ◆ Participates in advanced training and helps conduct introductory inservice programs.
- ◆ Trains new workers and serves as a positive role model and mentor.

Level-Two General Expectations

- ◆ Continues to meet expectations of Level One.
- ◆ Participates in inservice and continuing education programs.

- Serves as a positive role model and mentor—displays a positive attitude and is willing to help new workers.
- Actively pursues information that will help in personal and agency growth.
- Begins to demonstrate leadership skills.
- Initiates special events and innovative programs for youths and their families.

Level-One General Expectations

- Participates in and satisfactorily completes introductory inservice program and six-month probationary period.
- Follows procedures in the child and youth care policy manual.
- Demonstrates basic child and youth care skills.
- Is dependable and completes written assignments on time.
- Participates in team meetings and supervision and contributes to treatment planning decisions.

♦ be dependable and predictable;
♦ be creative;
♦ take risks;
♦ learn;
♦ communicate;
♦ be self-aware;
♦ solve problems;
♦ function as a team member; and
♦ make independent decisions.

Salaries

Akim and Natalie are paid about the same as teachers and social workers with similar amounts of experience. Since child and youth care work is valued equally with education and social work, an effort is made to compensate workers equally with members of those professions.

An effort is made to pay workers as much as members of other human service professions with equivalent amounts of education and experience. For example, a beginning worker with one year of experience and a bachelor's degree is paid the same as a beginning social worker or teacher with a bachelor's degree and one year of experience. Worker raises are equivalent to those in other human service professions and are based on performance and progression in the step system. If a decision is made to substitute life or work experience for education at the entry level (e.g., four years experience are equivalent to four years of education), then experience is rewarded the same as education.

Supportive Supervision, Leadership, and Mentoring

In addition to the mentorship she receives from Akim, Natalie has weekly supervision with Sue, who like Natalie, makes their meeting time a priority.

The step and promotion systems discussed earlier help create systems in which the most productive workers are on hand to be a role model for and mentor new workers. This process is one of encouragement, demonstration, and discussion. Workers lead and mentor one another as well as know where to go to seek advice and support. Sometimes mentors are assigned to new workers.

Workers receive at least one hour of individual supervision a week. With their supervisors they learn, solve problems, plan a career, and gain further self-awareness. Workers leave with added insight and enthusiasm for their jobs.

The supervisors have had experience as child and youth care workers and have prepared and trained to become supervisors. Team members also supervise and evaluate each other. Time is set aside at team meetings for workers to talk about individual and joint performance. Again, the purpose is to teach, solve problems, career plan, gain further self-awareness, and provide insight and support (see Chapter 3).

Schedules

Neither Akim nor Natalie expected to work regular hours when they took their jobs. Although some of their days are pretty long, they enjoy working hours that are different than the normal daily hours most of their friends work. They also find it easier to accept the hours they work because they are involved in helping make out the schedules.

Workers and supervisors together develop the daily working and vacation schedule, with the goal of having a balance of experienced and inexperienced workers on duty at all times. If there is room for choice of hours, it is given to senior workers first.

The objective is to always have a sufficient number of staff members on duty to ensure safety and a productive involvement.

The work week averages 40 hours. Except in emergencies, workers are not expected to work overtime. They are also given two to four weeks paid vacation and their time away from work is valued and respected.

Benefits

Natalie and Akim both feel reassured knowing that if they get sick, they will be able to pay for medical care. They also look forward to their vacations.

Health insurance is paid by the agency. Workers are assured that if they or members of their families become ill, they will receive proper medical treatment. Counseling services and leaves of absence are also provided for workers who are dealing with emotional stress.

Workers are also given paid vacation time so that they can take breaks from work. The work is simply too demanding not to get a break now and then.

Planning Time

Each week Natalie and Akim have in their schedules a few paid hours for planning.

This helps them to get ready and to be more effective in their activities and interactions.

To prevent problems and promote effective interaction, workers are allotted paid time for preparation. For instance, time is provided to write reports, to attend team and other decision-making meetings, and to participate in inservice training sessions. The agency's allotment of this time sends the message that worker input and participation is valued.

Awards and Recognition

Akim's picture is currently in the front lobby. He is worker of the month.

Workers are recognized for their achievements. In addition to daily doses of praise and encouragement, recognition includes worker-of-the-month awards, bonuses, articles in agency newsletters, and recognition dinners and ceremonies.

Making Decisions

Akim and Sue encourage Natalie to be engaged in the decision making processes at the agency. Not only did they value her insight, they also knew she would feel better about implementing plans she helped decide.

The door is open for workers to engage in decision making. With colleagues, administrators, and members of other professions, workers make decisions regarding the individual care of children as well as decisions that determine how the organization operates. Their involvement is supported and encouraged with supervision and training.

3

TEAM AND INDIVIDUAL INTERACTIONS

Teamwork has been a popular concept in child and youth care for many years [Fulcher 1981; Garner 1988, 1995; Vander Ven 1979], because workers who are members of teams tend to be more satisfied, committed, and effective than those who are not [Krueger 1986]. Teamwork, however, is not easy to achieve. It takes time, patience, commitment, training, and supervision.

Effective team members share common beliefs and values about working with children and families, and are committed to what they do. They have a sense of purpose or cause, and a feeling that what they do is important. These feelings are played out in their day-to-day interactions.

Further, effective team members are invested in their work and responsibilities. They can depend on and count on one another. They recognize the connection between their interactions with one another and their interactions with children, families, and communities. In other words, they realize that when they work well together, they are more likely to work well with children and families.

In trying to improve their interactions, effective team members use many of the skills they learned for building relationships. They lead, respond positively to leadership and others, and supervise each other. They serve as models and mentors. They listen to, praise, encourage, and positively confront one another. They willingly take risks to expand their experience. They are open and honest. They work at creating an atmosphere in which they can express their feelings. They have empathy for their colleagues, yet hold one another accountable.

In general, a satisfying team atmosphere is promoted by policies and actions such as the following [Krueger 1987b]:

1. The organization's philosophy of care and treatment is supported by of all members of the organization. To ensure that this occurs, the philosophy is periodically re-

viewed and altered according to the consensus views of members of the organization and the latest thinking about caring for children and families. It is difficult to work effectively as a member of a team in an organization if one's beliefs and values are not consistent with the philosophy of the organization.

2. As many decisions as possible are made by consensus. Team members compromise and strive to find an acceptable direction. They realize that in order to effectively carry out a decision, they must all be behind the decision. When consensus can't be reached, team members accept the decision of the majority or leadership and work hard to consistently carry it out.

3. Strong leadership is provided during team discussions and consensus-building sessions. The team leader follows the agenda and also allows room for questions and responses. He or she guides the discussion. If the discussion is moving away from the topic at hand, the leader moves the team members back on track. When consensus can't be reached, the leader makes a decision with the expectation that team members will respect and follow the decision.

4. Organizational leaders (executive directors, department heads, supervisors, etc.)

model teamwork among themselves. They set the tone for teamwork in the agency by working together. They develop policies by consensus and are consistent in implementing these policies.

5. Meetings are scheduled so that everyone has an equal opportunity to participate in making decisions. Encouragement and opportunities to speak are provided.

6. When, for financial, political, or some other significant reason, a consensus decision is overturned by the leadership, an explanation is given to staff in an effort to reach a mutual understanding. For example, an agency might decide to accept a new child when members of the team have decided it might not be the best time. When team members understand the financial, political, and therapeutic reasons for having their decision overturned, they often can accept the leader's decision.

7. Techniques of effective communication are practiced rigorously and modeled continuously. Team members use many of the same techniques among themselves that they use to help children and families.

8. Team members build a climate of support. They praise and encourage each other and confront one another with an underlying message of support and respect.

9. There is a system of accountability in which each team member understands how he or she is doing in moving toward personal and organizational goals. Team members are supervised and held accountable by one another as well as by the team leader.

10. Team members promote the development of skills such as the ability to:

♦ accept and give criticism;

♦ compromise to achieve consensus decisions;

♦ be assertive in advocating in behalf of children and families;

♦ be consistent in implementing team decisions;

♦ act independently without undermining the team;

♦ give and receive support and encouragement;

♦ lean from mistakes; and

♦ articulate positions and observations.

A Team Conversation

The conversation that follows is an example of the struggles and successes in effective teamwork:

Team members Bonny (the team leader), Mary, Nick, Al, and Tom are sitting in the office in a circle. Outside, a colleague is supervising a group of adolescents on the playground.

"I don't think he should go to the hockey game with us tonight," Mary says.

"Why not?" Nick asks.

"The way he's been behaving, he doesn't deserve it."

"I agree. He hasn't completed any of his tasks or routines, and he's gotten into at least two fights that I know about," Al says, supporting Mary's position.

"But I thought we agreed that these activities were part of his development," Nick says.

"Yes, we did," Bonny says.

"I don't understand," Mary says and leans back in her seat.

"Well, why would we want to deprive him of something that is beneficial to his social growth, if that's what he's here for," Nick responds.

"It's like our group meetings. They aren't rewards that can be given or taken away. The boys don't have to earn the right to participate," Bonny says.

"Well, I think he perceives hockey as a reward," Al says.

"Does he though? How would he perceive being left behind again?" Nick asks.

Tom, the newest team member, is listening but looks confused. Bonny notices and explains, "We believe that supervised activities are an integral part of the children's care and learning. Therefore, we try not to allow them to miss these activities."

"The more I think about it, Nick, I guess you're right," Mary says. "I remember when we had this discussion about how important it was for the kids to attend the support group, even if they weren't behaving very well." She pauses. "It's just that I get so frustrated when I can't manage his behavior."

"I know what you mean," Nick says.

Al seems deep in thought.

"Are you concerned about safety?" Bonny asks Al.

"Yes, partially, I guess, but if you all feel positive about it, I'm willing to give it a try. What Mary said makes sense."

"I appreciate your concern, Al. I share it," Bonny says, then looks at Nick. "You'll help supervise tonight, won't you?"

"Yes, of course," Nick answers. "And I'll be talking to him about his behavior, the same as the rest of you."

"Okay, then I think we should give it a try." Bonny's eyes circle the table and each team member either nods or voices approval. She glances at her watch and con-

tinues, "There are only a few minutes left. Let's check in with each other. How's everyone doing?"

"Good," Mary says.

"Yes, there are nights when I feel like I've had it, but in general I feel pretty good about things," Al says.

"I'm feeling good about the kids and families. And about us," Nick says.

Bonny looks over at Tom, the newest worker. "It's a little early for you, I know, Tom, but how is it going?"

Tom thinks for a moment, then looks at Bonny. "Well, it's been pretty rough. The kids have really tested me. Without all your support, I don't know if I'd have made it." He looks at everyone around the table.

"We understand how difficult it is when you first start," Al says and tells Tom about how one of the kid's put sugar in his gas line when he was new. "Since then I've had a lock on my gas cap," Al concludes, laughing.

"Please continue to ask for help whenever you need it, Tom," Bonny says.

"I will," Tom responds.

The following week...

On the way to the next team meeting, Jane, a new worker, walks through the recreation

area with Al. Children run by, playing.
"Walk!" Al shouts.

Jane listens intently as he points out how
the children are expected to behave in the
recreation room, taking in as much as she
can. When they arrive at the meeting, the
others are already present and talking.

"I like the way you closed up last night,
Al," Mary says. "The place looked good today."

"Thanks, they were all talking about what
a good time they had on your outing."

They sit and begin moving smoothly
through the agenda. As Al speaks, Mary
leans forward, giving him eye contact.
Bonny nods. Nick begins to say something,
then waits until Al is finished. Mary smiles.

"It's important that we all follow through
with praising Jimmy each time he completes
a chore," Al says.

"Yes, I've got to remember that," Tom
says.

A few weeks later...

At the team meeting, the discussion focuses
on Ned, a challenging youth.

I don't think he belongs here," Al says.

"Yeah, whenever he's here, he takes up
most of my time," Mary adds.

"His parents don't care. They want us to baby-sit," Nick says.

"Yeah, his constant acting out ruins it for the rest of the group. I'm afraid to go anywhere," Tom says.

"I think we should take a look at what's going on here," Bonny observes.

"What do you mean?" Mary asks.

"It's related, isn't it?"

Nick nods knowingly.

"I'm not sure what you're getting at," Al says, looking confused.

"What often happens in dysfunctional families?" Bonny asks.

"The parents want to push their kid out or give him to us and expect us to fix him up," Nick responds.

"Exactly. And what are we doing?"

"Pushing out Ned," Al says.

"Okay, now let's explore some alternatives. What are Ned's strengths?" Bonny asks. They all think a moment.

"Al, he seems to seek you out," Bonny says.

"Yeah, he likes to play one-on-one basketball. He's good."

"Maybe we can get him on an intramural team," Mary says.

"I'll make another effort to get to his parent's home," Nick says.

Later, at an administrative meeting...

Bonny meets with the other team leaders and the executive director.

"I've been thinking about having an administrative retreat," the executive director says to the team leaders.

"I like that idea," one of the other team leaders says.

"I do too, but why not invite the entire staff?" Bonny asks.

"Wouldn't it be better if we ironed out our differences first?" Bill says.

"If we're supposed to model teamwork, why not have the staff be a part of the process. It would be good for us to work things through together," Bonny responds.

"You have a good point, Bonny," the executive director says.

"Maybe it will work," Bill says. "How would we structure it?"

"At your next team meetings, ask the staff members what they think. Try to identify the three or four issues or ideas that we ought to be addressing. Then we'll come back together and tease out the most common ones. Those will form our agenda for the day."

"Sounds good," Bonny says.

The following day...

One of the girls asks Tom how old he was when he first had sex. He raises the issue of his reaction at a team meeting.

"What did you say?" Bonny asks.

"That I didn't think it was proper for me to share that kind of information. But later I felt as if I was defensive."

"It's hard to know how much to share with these kids," Al says.

"Yeah, you want to be open, the way you want them to be, but it's awkward," Mary says.

"Most of the issues surrounding sex, drugs, and loss are tough," Bonny says. "Maybe we should practice here a little bit."

"Good idea, I often wonder how to handle those situations myself, "Nick says

"Why don't we role play? Tom, com'on over here and sit across from Mary." Bonny says, seizing the opportunity for training.

That night...

Jane walks beside Al as they leave work.

"Do you think Mary was upset when I agreed with you earlier," Jane asks.

"No, but if you think she was, you should talk to her about it," Al says.

Jane starts to say something, then pauses. "You're right, I have to be direct."

Al smiles.

Satisfying Interactions with Children and Youths

Nadia, a youth worker, comes to the group home early to go jogging with Carlos, who is ready and waiting when she arrives. After they've gone a few blocks and warmed up, they run easily together over the curbs and uneven surfaces of the street.

Nick, a youth worker, and Anton, a youth, kick the soccer ball back and forth. They chase after the ball as if connected by their enthusiasm.

Latisha is in the arts and crafts room with four girls and two boys from her group. They are working with clay, kneading it with their hands and creating whatever shapes and forms come to mind. She moves from one youth to the other, asking for their interpretation and giving hers. The room fills with friendly laughter.

Maria, the youth worker, passes the bowl of french fries to Tom, one of the boys at the group home. Her smile and the friendly movement of her arm set in motion a series of similar actions.

Hank, the youth worker, sits on the couch reading a magazine; in the room are five boys, who are also reading. A couple of the boys are on the floor. One is next to him on the couch and the other two are sitting at a table by the window. Music plays in the background.

Satisfaction for most workers is found in the daily interactions and connections such as those described above. Although it is beyond the scope of this book to cover all the major elements that lead to successful interactions, it is noteworthy that workers' stories about and description of these moments usually include four central themes: rhythm, presence, meaning, and atmosphere. These themes are described in the excerpts from *Nexus: A Book About Youth Work* [Krueger 1995] that follow.*

Rhythm

Rhythm is beat, motion, tempo. Workers and youth moving through the day in and out of synch—a series of upbeats and down-

---

* The sections on rhythm, presence, meaning and atmosphere are reprinted with permissions from M. Krueger, *Nexus: A book about youth work* (Milwaukee, WI: University Outreach Press), pp. 2–6.

beats. The movement of a group of teenagers from one activity to the next at an easy pace. A discussion of what is to come (foreshadowing) conducted in a firm, reassuring voice. The movement of hands mirroring the flow of the moment.

A steady tone of voice that calms rather than excites; or a staccato, jubilant voice encouraging youth to participate in an activity.

A body positioned and moving to quell an attack or provide a safe zone of expression. A nonthreatening hand reaching out to assist. A "quick step" and a grasp to avoid being hit.

"Have you noticed that when people jog, dance or throw a frisbee in rhythm with each other, they seem to experience momentary bonding and a sense of unity? At these and other moments of joint rhythmic engagement, they discover an attraction for each other, whether there has been a previous sense of caring. In fact, it is almost impossible not to like a person while being rhythmically in sync." [Maier 1992: 7]

Presence

Workers often speak of the need to be "real." Presence ... seems to come as much from the quest to understand oneself as it does from the amount of awareness and skill in expressing self one has. A person who is searching to know himself or herself is more real than one who is not. The search is part of who one is, however, not necessarily a constant process of conscious self-examination. People who are consumed by self are not present.

Presence is also being there with conviction and the knowledge that children who have been physically and psychologically abandoned throughout their lives need committed, dependable, predictable adults whom they can count on...

Fewster [1991] teaches that youth work is a shared journey: worker and youth going through the day searching and trying to discover themselves. In the journey, the worker, who is the more experienced traveler, leads by being present and aware until eventually the youth finds his or her own path.

Presence is also being *with* children and families:

"Youth workers... don't build trust mechanically, like carpenters build houses: they are in the world with youth and, in so being, disclose trust as fundamental to being together as persons." [Baizerman 1992: 132]

Presence is conveyed by eyes, smiles and nods that are alert and attentive. By an honest expression of how one feels. By listening intently, with eye contact and feedback. By showing up for work on time. By enthusiasm during activities and routines. By being predictable and dependable.

It is also conveyed by expressions of self-confidence and the will to hang in there during a crisis. By firmness. By the conscious and unconscious quest to know oneself. By a quiver of the voice that alerts a worker to an unresolved issue or underlying fear. By awareness of how one's feelings about abandonment, attachment, success, and failure influence one's interactions and the ability to adjust one's actions accordingly to meet the needs of youth who have been severely abused and have experienced considerable abandonment and rejection. By using this awareness of self to be more aware of and sensitive to others' feelings. By the underlying message: we can move forward together, you and I. I am confident based on my experience and knowledge of your needs that we can make it. You are safe, because I am here and will go with you. I will try to know myself if you will try to know yourself.

Meaning

Bruner [1990] argues that in order to understand humans, we have to understand how experiences and acts are shaped by intentional states and that the form of these intentional states is realized through participation in the symbolic systems of culture.

> *Indeed, the very shape of our lives—the rough and changing draft of our autobiography that we carry in our minds—is understandable to ourselves and others only by those cultural systems of interpretation. [Bruner 1990: 33]*

In ... [child and youth care], meaning can be defined as acting with purpose in the context of one's cultural or familial or social experience. A way of moving, a gesture, a spoken word, a ritual or a way of solving a problem that has meaning within one's past or present family, group, community life. It is also the meaning arrived at through what has been referred to as a mutually constructed reality or the common ground that is sometimes needed for two or more people to communicate and solve problems. Meaning is also the sense of two people who are acting together with a positive purpose, even if the purpose or meaning of the action is different for each participant.

A worker or youth acts because he or she believes it is right to act and that the actions will bring fulfillment for oneself as well as others. A worker and youth find a common purpose and act together because they believe it is best. A worker or youth acts because the actions create something that feels familiar or good or safe. A piece of bread buttered, a collar buttoned or unbuttoned, a phrase delivered, a ball batted, or a fork held in a certain way because it evokes these feelings. Or perhaps a problem is resolved or an effort undertaken in a way that one believes will lead to the best results.

A sense of meaning or purpose is conveyed by workers to youths and often vice versa through actions and words. Through reframing a situation so that there is common, or acceptance of different, purpose. Through contentment or joy or enthusiasm. Through conviction. Through confidence that what one is doing is wholesome and good. Through actions that are consistent with the intended purpose. Through the message: We are doing this together, with meaning, you and I. The process and the outcome of our actions will be fruitful. I understand that it might have a different meaning for you, but I hope and believe it will be fulfilling.

Atmosphere

Atmosphere is space, time, surroundings. It is also tone and mood. Maier [1987] writes that the space we create defines us and helps bring people together, to be in touch with and aware of each other, and to engage in parallel activities. He also writes that space provides distance when needed.

Atmosphere, of course, can enhance most interactions. A light turned down to quiet the group. A radio turned up to invigorate. Rooms decorated with children's paintings and posters to encourage expression and to help provide a sense of safety and familiarity. Reds, blues, and yellows to liven things up. Earth tones to ground. Chairs placed in a circle to facilitate discussion and participation. A room or hallway sized properly for an activity. A window left open or closed for comfort.

Workers also create atmosphere with the tones of their voices. The expressions on their faces. A mood that sends off good vibes. A sense of being and confidence that evokes permanence and safety. We are in this space, you and I, and together we create, change and shape it for our mutual benefit.

Themes and Moments

These themes seem to run through satisfying interactions and moments. For example, workers who are experiencing these moments are present. They are with children and youths, growing and learning together. They are also acting with meaning or purpose. In most instances, there is also a sense of rhythm or shared movement. Worker and youth or child are in synch. The atmosphere (e.g., tone, mood, and surroundings) also enhances the interaction.

In this context, satisfying child and youth care work is a process of self in action. The worker striving to enhance his or her effectiveness and satisfaction asks:

Am I present? Have I brought myself to the moment? Is what we are doing meaningful? Is there something else we can do that will have a more fulfilling purpose? Are we in synch? How is the space and my mood contributing or detracting from successful interaction?

4

CAREER AND PROFESSIONAL DEVELOPMENT

Alicia goes to school part time and attends child and youth care association meetings and conferences where she meets and works with other people who are trying to build careers in the field. Her goal is to someday have her own group home.

Phil, who has several years experience as a youth worker, has been conducting inservice training sessions at his agency. Last month, he got his master's degree with a focus on child and youth care. He wants to go on to get his doctorate, then teach child and youth care at a university. The agency where he works will continue to pay an increasing percentage of his tuition as long as he stays with them.

Marsha goes to every inservice training she can on families. Someday, she wants to work in the agency's in-home service program.

Tony is almost finished with his bachelor's degree. He's been leading a few team meetings. His supervisor feels he has potential to become a supervisor some day.

A number of workers have managed to carve out successful careers in the child and youth care field [Vander Ven 1981, 1990]. By seizing the opportunities available in the emerging child and youth care profession, they have found doors open that are often shut in more established professions (see appendix for a list of organizations and universities that provide career and educational opportunities). Following are four examples of workers who have been successful in building a career.

Martina

A teacher whom she admired very much had convinced Martina that child and youth care was a fulfilling career. So she decided to study it in school. While earning her bachelor's degree in social work, she focused much of her attention on children and families. She also completed a field placement at a residential treatment center, where she experienced child and youth care firsthand. The staff were pleased with her work, and after she graduated, she was hired as a full-time youth worker.

She adjusted fairly quickly and became effective with the most difficult of the adolescent boys. They seemed to sense her resolve and did not challenge her authority the way they challenged some of the other workers.

When she was on duty, there was always plenty for the boys to do. She was always involved with them in one activity of another: cooking, baseball, chores, and group meetings.

As she gained experience in her job, she became more and more aware of the importance of families. After leaving the treatment center, many of the boys regressed because their families had not changed. And it was clear that some boys could have stayed home if their parents would have had more help. So Martina began to think about how she could develop a program to help families change. In her third year at the agency, she went back to graduate school part-time and focused her studies on family work and policy.

After graduation she developed a proposal for a new family-based program. The county social service agency funded it. She called it Intensive In-Home Services and hired two youth workers to help with it. As a team, they went to the homes of troubled children and helped their family members, gearing their interventions to the needs of each family. If one family needed a youth worker there at breakfast or bedtime, a worker was there teaching and helping the parents at those and other times. Another family might need several hours of counseling. The goal was to give families as much help as possible and empower them to identify and solve their own problems.

Eventually the program grew to be one of the most successful in the state, and Martina spent many years doing what she liked—working directly with youth and families. After retiring, she was in demand as a consultant and teacher.

Lori

Lori liked working with street kids. She had a degree in psychology and had worked in group care, but she found her place when she started working the street. There was something about the unpredictability of interaction and intensity of need that appealed to her. It became a major part of her life, being on the streets talking with kids who had problems with gangs, pimps, drugs, and abusive parents. She was good at thinking on her feet and solving crises. A natural, one could say.

After working for a storefront organization, she decided to go into business for herself. She talked the county into letting her use her residence as a shelter for kids, who could stay under her supervision for a day or period of days until a more permanent situation was established. Some kids came back often, others she never saw again.

Lori was also a good teacher. Organizations often called her to conduct training workshops. She was respected for her commitment, grit, and practical knowledge. Youth workers, like youths, could relate to her lessons. She was offered other jobs that paid more, but she liked what she did and the independence of working for herself.

Matt

When he was in high school, Matt worked at summer camps and playgrounds. He liked working with kids, but in college he decided to study business because that was where he thought the money was. It didn't take him long to realize he had made the wrong decision. Shortly after starting a job for an insurance company, he began to miss working with young people.

He quit his job and applied for a job as a night watchman at a residential treatment center, thinking this would give him the income and time in the day he needed to go back to school in human development. But after his interview, he was offered a job as a child and youth care worker instead.

The job was very difficult at first. The children challenged and tested him. On many nights, Matt questioned himself and the choice he had made. Fortunately, however, he had supportive colleagues who helped him through the rough times.

In his second year at the agency, Matt attended a Child and Youth Care Association meeting and met workers from other agencies who had come together to learn and to promote the professional development of the field. In addition to increasing his knowledge and meeting other professionals, his involvement in association activities also taught him about the emerging national profession. He began to realize that perhaps there were other possibilities for his future—although as far as he was concerned, he could stay at his agency working with the kids indefinitely.

His work with the children was evaluated by his supervisor. He learned from these evaluations and continued to build on his strengths and weaknesses. He ran for and was elected president of the state child and youth care association. He also returned to school to get a master's degree in human development with a focus on child and youth care. Whenever possible, he attended conferences and workshops, eventually submitting his own proposal to do a workshop. It was accepted.

Matt enjoyed writing about his experience. When he learned that child and youth care journals were looking for contributions from practitioners, he submitted an article. When it was published, he received positive feedback from his peers across the country.

At the end of his fifth year, Matt was promoted to child and youth care supervisor, another challenging, growth-producing experience. He struggled until he learned how to apply to the staff members he supervised many of the methods of care he used elsewhere in his work. From the beginning, however, he served as a positive role model.

Matt finished his master's degree and con-

tinued to work toward a Ph.D. He re-
searched innovative approaches to child
and youth care. As he neared the comple-
tion of his doctorate, he decided that he
would like to teach what he had learned to
other youth care workers and students who
wanted to go into youth care work. As one
of only a few Ph.D.s in child and youth care,
he found a job as a faculty member at one
of many universities that were beginning to
develop child and youth care-related
courses. His experience and education
served him well as he took on the role of
teacher.

Arnie

When Arnie retired from the military in his
mid-forties, he took a continuing education
course in youth work. He had several interviews before he decided to accept an offer
at a facility with a strong outdoor program.
He loved to camp and thought this would
be a good way to work with youths from the
city.

At first, Arnie had to learn how to balance
discipline with care. His military experience
had taught him how to provide structure,
but it had not prepared him for emotionally disturbed youths who defied authority.
His supervisor helped him understand the

differences between these young people and the young men with whom he had worked in the military. The supervisor also helped him understand what it meant to a youth to be emotionally disturbed and showed him how to be patient and to set realistic expectations.

The kids in the program liked being with Arnie, because they knew that beneath his stern exterior he really cared for and enjoyed being with them. He was always teaching them how to do something—pitch a tent, paddle a canoe, build a fire, etc. And as he learned to set firm limits without ordering them around, they began to learn and comply with his limits.

Arnie continued to take courses and workshops whenever he could. He wanted to learn as much as he could about youth work. He had experienced much in life, but for him there was nothing more rewarding than singing around a campfire in the woods with young people.

Arnie stayed on as a youth worker for 20 years before he retired; even after he retired, he came in often to volunteer his time.

Nathan

Nathan heard about the Peace Corps in college and signed up after he graduated.

When he returned to the states after working with children in Central America, he found a job at a group home where the Spanish he had learned overseas came in handy, as did his experience working with Nicaraguan children.

Soon Nathan became a leader at the group home. He was always engaged with the children in activities and eager to help his colleagues. They knew they could count on him—he rarely missed a day's work.

Nathan was also instrumental in helping the agency become more treatment oriented. He had read books about the therapeutic milieu and studied methods of counseling in his special education courses, and had previously applied his knowledge in the Peace Corps. He taught other staff members how to turn crises into successful therapeutic and learning encounters. Even the agency psychologists were impressed by his insight and skill.

After several years at the group home, Nathan went back to school part-time to earn a master's degree in a new youth work program that had been developed at a nearby university. It was a challenge going to school and working full-time but he was convinced that the additional knowledge would enhance his work and his career.

School was also more relevant now that he had such rich experiences in the field.

He continued on for his doctorate and eventually was hired as the director of a series of group homes, where he quickly developed therapeutic, caring environments for some of the city's most challenging youths. He was an active director and spent many hours with the residents and modeling youth work for the staff. Several workers soon wanted to follow in his footsteps.

Characteristics of Workers with Successful Careers

In talking with and reviewing the careers of successful professionals, several factors become evident:

1. These professionals had a vision. Early in their careers, they realized child and youth care was where they wanted to be and they pursued educational, performance, and professional goals that would help them reach their goals.

2. They made good choices about the places they worked. Most recall their initial experiences fondly. They can remember many positive lessons they learned and friends they made.

3. Realizing the importance of being there for children and families and the time it took to become proficient at their work, they maintained their commitments to the agencies that employed them.

4. They worked hard and developed a strong performance record.

5. They found good mentors and learned as much as they could from them.

6. They had supervisors and mentors who steered them toward educational programs and career options.

7. They attended conferences, workshops, and professional association meetings that kept them abreast of the latest methods of practice. This also put them in touch with other professionals, who also had a vision and access to information about future employment opportunities.

8. They realized early on that it was important to get as much formal education as possible.

9. They continued to educate themselves throughout their careers, either by continuing their course work or through disciplined reading and self-study.

10. Based on an assessment of their skills, abilities, and aptitude, which began early in their careers, they identified a career track to pursue. Some chose to stay in direct service, while others decided to move into supervision, administration, or child and youth care education.

Professional Development

Many workers find satisfaction in being involved in something beyond their agency that enhances their work and the lives of children. An emerging profession, child and youth care provides many opportunities for such involvement [Krueger 1991]. Members of the field have made remarkable progress in organizing, setting standards, developing education programs, and advocating for children (see appendix for a list of association addresses).

Career Tracks, Opportunities, and Enhancers

Like most other professions, child and youth care work today offers several career tracks and opportunities [Vander Ven 1981].

Direct Service

Most workers are in direct service. They spend much of their time interacting with children and youths in group or community centers. Although the incentives in comparison to other professions are still marginal, today there are more agencies than in the past with step systems and supportive atmospheres that offer workers financial incentives and growth opportunities.

Some workers have used their ingenuity and knowledge to develop their own programs. Others have gone into business for themselves, operating group homes, neighborhood centers, and family support programs in which they provide direct service.

Education

Since the early 1960s, hundreds of education and training programs have been developed for child and youth care workers [Vander Ven 1991]. Many state associations and universities have also developed continuing education programs that meet professional certification requirements.

This has created opportunities for teaching child and youth care. Some workers have earned advanced degrees and gone on to teach at colleges and universities. Others have augmented their careers by teaching courses or workshops at conferences. Some have created their own training or consulting businesses.

Administration

Many workers have also moved into administration. They have become supervisors and executive directors, or have taken jobs in government. Like those who have gone into teaching, most of these workers have earned advanced degrees.

Writing and Research

Writing and research by workers has been and is instrumental to the growth of the field. Child and youth care is now truly a profession with its own knowledge base [Krueger 1991]. Unlike many other professions, however, the doors for publishing and sharing one's work are still wide open. Each of the major journals listed in the appendix are seeking articles from child and youth care workers. Publishers are also willing to publish books for college courses and the growing number of practitioners who are trying to meet their training requirements. There are also dozens of newsletters seeking articles, stories, and essays from child and youth care workers. Many workers have seized these opportunities to share what they have learned and to add impressive achievements to their resumes.

Building a Career

For workers interested in building a career
in the field, it might be helpful to think
about integrating the material in this book
into the following action steps:

Get a Good Start

Give careful consideration to whether or not
you want to be a child and youth care
worker [Fewster 1991]. Search your heart
and soul.

If you decide to go ahead, then try to make
a good initial job choice. Workers remember their earliest experiences, and these
tend to shape their attitudes toward the
field. During interviews, ask questions to
see if the organization has taken the steps
outlined in Chapter 2. When you accept a

job, learn as much as you can from your peers and in training. Identify your sources of satisfaction and actively pursue interactions that will make you happy.

Keep Commitments and Work Hard

It usually takes at least a year to get a feel for the work and two years to master some of the basics. Two years is also longer than children stay involved in most programs. To learn and to assure the children that you won't leave before many of them do, be prepared to make at least a two-year commitment, then do everything possible to keep it. Work hard! Few workers who bounce from one program to another succeed.

Start to Know Yourself

Learn from yourself and your experience. Get a sense of your strengths and weaknesses. Seek input from supervisors and colleagues. Understand how your beliefs and values influence your interactions.

As you learn about your strengths and weaknesses, begin to think about tracks and career growth. Will you stay in direct care? Move into teaching? Become an administrator? What skills will you need? How can you improve—or obtain—these skills?

Join an Association

Get engaged in activities outside the agency. Join a professional association of workers (see appendix) and begin attending conferences and workshops. Often, workers learn about new opportunities at these events. Being part of something beyond one's agency also provides an additional source of energy and inspiration. Work with others to promote competent care.

Continue to Learn

Seize opportunities inside and outside the agency for learning. Learn from team and individual interactions in service programs and at conferences. Go back to school. Gear your studies to the career track you have chosen. For example, if you plan on staying in direct service, take courses in human development, counseling, and recreation. If you want to move into training, take education courses. And, if you want to be an administrator, take administration courses. Knowledge is power.

Propose Change

Be a leader. Initiate change with constructive, well thought-out proposals. Use your insight and ingenuity to make the agency more effective.

Develop a Strong Performance Record

Be aware of your performance objectives, then focus as much on how you achieve an objective as on reaching it. Few workers advance or are satisfied without a total commitment to doing as well as they can.

Renew Your Commitment Along the Way

Periodically stop to think about why you are in child and youth care. Keep the fire in your belly burning.

REFERENCES AND SUGGESTED READINGS

Anglin, J., Denholm, C., Furgeson, R., & Pence, A. (Eds.). (1990). *Perspectives in professional child and youth care: Part I.* New York: Haworth Press.

Austin, D., & Halpin, B. (1989). The caring response. *Journal of Child and Youth Care,* 4(3), 1–7.

Baizerman, M. (1992). Book review of *Buckets: Sketches from a youthworker's log book,* by Mark Krueger (1990). *Child and Youth Care Forum,* 21(2), 129–133.

Beker, J. (1991). An interview. *Journal of Child and Youth Care Work,* 7, 40–43.

Brendtro, L. (1991). An interview. *Journal of Child and Youth Care Work,* 7, 44–46

Bronfenbrenner, U. (1979). *The ecology of human development*. Cambridge, MA: Harvard University Press.

Bruner, J. (1990). *Acts of meaning*. Cambridge, MA: Harvard University Press.

Cohen, G. (1990). Vera. In M. Krueger & N. Powell (Eds.), *Choices in caring: Contemporary approaches to child and youth care work*. Washington, DC: Child Welfare League of America.

Felicetti, T. (1987). Convincing care staff to use their selves. *Residential Treatment for Children and Youth, 5*(2), 59–60.

Fewster, G. (1990). *Being in child care: A journey into self*. New York: Haworth, 1990.

Fewster, G. (1991). The paradoxical journey: Some thoughts on relating to children. *Journal of Child and Youth Care, 6*(4), v–ix.

Fulcher, L. (1981). Team functioning in group care. In F. Ainsworth & L. Fulcher (Eds.), *Group care for children*. New York: Tavistock.

Garner, H. (1988). *Helping others through teamwork*. Washington, DC: Child Welfare League of America.

Garner, H. (Ed.). (1995). *Teamwork models*

and experiences in education and child and youth care. Needham Heights, MA: Allyn and Bacon.

Havel, V. (1982). *Letters to Olga.* New York: Henry Holt and Co.

Krueger, M. (1986). *Job satisfaction for child and youth care workers.* Washington, DC: Child Welfare League of America.

Krueger, M. (1987). *Floating.* Washington, DC: Child Welfare League of America.

Krueger, M. (1987b). Making the team approach work. *Child Welfare, 66,* 447–458.

Krueger, M., Lauerman, R., Beker, J., Savicki, V., Parry, P., & Powell, N. (1987). Professional child and youth care work in the United States and Canada: A report of the NOCCWA Research and Study Committee. *Journal of Child and Youth Care Work, 3*(1), 19–31.

Krueger, M. (1990). *In motion.* Washington, DC: Child Welfare League of America.

Krueger, M. (1991). *Buckets: Sketches from a youthworker's log book.* Washington, DC: Child Welfare League of America.

Krueger, M. (1991). A review and analysis of the development of professional child and youth care work. *Child and Youth Care Forum, 20*(6), 379–389.

Krueger, M. (1994). Framing child and youth care in moments of rhythm, presence, meaning, and atmosphere. *Child and Youth Care Forum*, (23)5, 325–331.

Krueger, M. (1995). Using care to improve effectiveness. *Child and Youth Care Administrator*, 6(1), 35–37.

Krueger, M. (1995). *Nexus: A book about youth work*. Milwaukee: Outreach Press.

Krueger, M., & Drees, M. (1995). Generic teamwork. In H. Garner (Ed.), *Teamwork models and experiences in education and child and youth care*. Needham Heights, MA: Allyn and Bacon.

Long, N. (1991). An interview. *Journal of Child and Youth Care Work*, 7, 49.

Maier, H. (1991). An interview. *Journal of Child and Youth Care Work*, 7, 51–54.

Maier, H. (1987). *Developmental group care of children and youth*. New York: Haworth.

Maier, H. (1992). Rhythmicity—A powerful force for experiencing unity and personal connections. *Journal of Child and Youth Care Work*, 8, 7–13.

Mattingly, M. (1977). Sources of stress and burnout in child care. *Child Care Quarterly*, 6(2).

Meyer, M. J. (1991). Troubled children teach us a lot about ourselves. *Journal of Child and Youth Care Work,* 7, 81–94.

Nault, S. (1987). Maybe I'm not cut out to be a child care worker after all. *Journal of Child and Youth Care Work,* 3, 81–86.

Nguyen, P. (1992). Journal at the shelter. *Child and Youth Care Forum,* 21(2), 91–104.

Porter, L., Steers, R., Boulian, P., & Mowday, R. (1974). Organizational commitment, job satisfaction, and turnover among psychiatric technicians. *Journal of Applied Psychology,* 59, 151–176.

Vander Ven, K. (1979). Towards maximum effectiveness of the unit team approach in residential care. *Residential and Community Child Care Administration,* I(3), 287–297.

Vander Ven, K. (1981). Patterns of career development in group care. In F. Ainsworth & L. Fulcher (Eds.), *Group care for children.* New York: Tavistock.

Vander Ven, K. (1990). Origins of my career in child and youth care work: The 4 C's pathway. *Journal of Child and Youth Care Work,* 6, 68–79

Vander Ven, K., Mattingly, M., & Morris, M. (1982). Principles and guidelines for child care preparation programs. *Child Care Quarterly, 11*(3), 221–244.

Vander Ven, K., & Tittnich, E. (1986). *Competent caregivers, competent children: Training and education for child and youth care practice.* New York: Haworth.

Waggoner, C. (1984). First impressions. *Child and Youth Care Quarterly, 12*(4), 255–265.

Appendix

Career Information and Opportunities in Youth Work

Journals

Child and Youth Care Administrator
Fischler Center for Advancement of
    Education
NOVA/ Southeastern University
3301 College Avenue
Ft. Lauderdale, FL 33314

Child and Youth Care Forum
Youth Studies Program
University of Minnesota School of
    Social Work
386 McNeal Hall
1985 Buford Avenue
St. Paul, MN 55108

Journal of Child and Youth Care
University of Calgary Press
2500 University Drive
Calgary, Alberta T2N 1N4

Journal of Child and Youth Care Work
National Organization of Child Care
Worker Associations.
Child and Youth Care Learning Center
University of Wisconsin—Milwaukee
P.O. Box 413
Milwaukee, WI 53201

Newspaper

Youth Today
1200 17th Street, NW, 4th Floor
Washington, DC 20036

Newsletters

Child and Youth Care Work
(Publication of NOCCWA)
c/o Child and Youth Care Learning
Center
University of Wisconsin—Milwaukee
P.O. Box 413
Milwaukee, WI 53201

University Programs and Resource Centers

Child and Youth Care Learning Center
(Also headquarters for the National
Organization of Child
Care Worker Associations)
University of Wisconsin-Milwaukee
P.O Box 413
Milwaukee, WI 53201

Program in Child Care and Child Development
University of Pittsburgh School of
Social Work
Pittsburgh, PA 15261

Youth Studies Program
University of Minnesota School of
Social Work
386 McNeal Hall
1985 Buford Avenue
St. Paul, MN 55108

Master's Program in Child and Youth Care Administration, and Doctoral Program in Youth Studies
NOVA/Southeastern University
3301 College Ave
Ft. Lauderdale, FL 33314

The Trieschman Center
   1968 Central Ave.
   Needham MA 02912

Canada

School of Child and Youth Care
   University of Victoria
   P.O. Box 1700
   Victoria, BC, Canada, V8W 2Y2

School of Child and Youth Care
   Rhyerson Polytechnical Institute
   350 Victoria Street
   Toronto, ON, Canada M5B 2K3

About the Author

Mark Krueger, Ph.D., is a professor and director of the Child and Youth Care Learning Center, University of Wisconsin–Milwaukee. Prior to coming to the university, he was a child and youth care worker for 11 years. Among the other child and youth care books he has written are three textbooks, *Intervention Techniques for Child and Youth Care Workers, Careless to Caring for Troubled Youth,* and *Choices in Caring;* two novels, *Floating* and *In Motion*; and a book of short stories, *Buckets*. He has also contributed several articles to child and youth care journals, spoken at or conducted workshops at child and youth care conferences throughout the United States and Canada, and is past president of the National Organization of Child Care Worker Associations.